THE LIFE & TIMES OF

MARY QUEEN OF SCOTS

THE LIFE & TIMES OF

Mary Queen of Scots

BY
James Brown

This edition first published by
Parragon Book Service Ltd in 1996

Parragon Book Service Ltd
Unit 13–17 Avonbridge Trading Estate
Atlantic Road, Avonmouth
Bristol BS11 9QD

Produced by Magpie Books,
an imprint of Robinson Publishing

ISBN 0 75251 592 6

A copy of the British Library Cataloguing in Publication
Data is available from the British Library.

Typeset by Whitelaw & Palmer Ltd, Glasgow
Printed in Singapore

THE INFANT QUEEN

Her birth was the last of many disappointments that killed her father. James V, King of Scotland, had a turbulent neighbour in the portly person of Henry VIII, King of England. Henry coveted a military reputation, and to that end, whenever his coffers and the labyrinthine diplomatic politics of Europe permitted, he would invade France in an attempt to recover the French lands which English Kings had once held. However, if he went to

France with an army he had to be sure that the King of Scotland would not follow a traditional course of action and swoop down upon an unguarded England. This pattern was repeated in 1542. Henry embarked on a costly, and ultimately futile, escapade in France, at the same time sending the Duke of Norfolk north with another force to tackle the Scottish threat. As it turned out, the Scottish expedition was the greater success. James was comprehensively defeated at Solway Moss. He escaped from the battlefield with his life, and took to his bed declaring that he would never rise more. News arrived that his French wife had borne him a child: a daughter. In an age when dynastic considerations weighed heavily, and getting sons was vital for a king, this was the last straw. He turned his face to the wall, and, thinking of how his family had originally

James V of Scotland

gained the crown through a woman, foretold the end of the Stewarts: 'The Devil go with it. It came with a lass and will go with a lass.' Six days later he died. His baby daughter Mary became Queen of Scotland.

Between Scotland and France there was an old friendship, founded largely on their shared suspicions of England. Over the next few years Scottish politics would be dominated by the international tension between England and France, with the whole situation complicated by the politics of religion. The reformed church was struggling to establish itself in Scotland. The monarchs involved also had dynastic motives to consider. The infant Mary was already being sought as a bride. Henry VIII wanted her to marry his son, Edward, and to ensure the success of this plan, he was eager to get control of her. In 1547 the Dowager Queen and her daughter were sheltering in Stirling Castle. There the child Queen had sat in the chair of state while her lords and chieftains swore allegiance to her. That September they heard that the English had inflicted a defeat on the Scots at the battle of Pinkie Cleugh, and were advancing on the castle. In the dead of night Mary was hastened to safety on the island of Inchmahome.

In the midst of this turmoil a possibility presented itself to the Dowager Queen to secure her daughter's future. After long being infertile, Catherine de' Medici, the Italian wife of Henry, Dauphin of France, had given birth to a boy, Francis, in 1543. When his grandfather, King Francis, died in 1547 (in the same year as Henry VIII), this little boy became the Dauphin, and his father became Henry II. It seemed to some that the ideal way to cement the Franco-Scottish alliance would be to marry Queen Mary to the Dauphin. That she was only five and he was younger was no great obstacle. A marriage agreement was signed and Mary was carried in some state to France to begin a new life, while her mother stayed to wrestle with the intractable problems of Scottish politics. For the greater part of Mary's minority, her mother governed Scotland.

Mary arrived in France in 1548. Her mother's family, the Guises, immediately took her under their wing. After the royal family, the Valois, the Guises were the most powerful family in France. In this young member of the clan they saw the chance to make themselves

Mary of Guise

more powerful still. She was already Queen of
Scotland; in due course she would marry the
Dauphin and become Queen of France. But
most of all she was a Guise, and, if properly
brought up, would serve the interests of the
family.

Her uncles, Francis and Charles, Cardinal of
Lorraine, and her grandmother, the Duchess,
looked to her education. Through her they
hoped one day to control France. The early
signs were favourable. The Dauphin was
sickly, and swiftly developed an affection
amounting almost to dependency for Mary.
The two children were brought up together
at court.

In 1558 their marriage was celebrated. It was
a glorious occasion. So many wanted to see

the ceremony that, rather than perform it inside the cathedral of Notre Dame, it was performed on the steps in full view of the crowds. The royal party then proceeded to a lavish banquet and a ball, the climax of which was a masque of elaborate model galleons, each containing a prince, and sailing about the ballroom floor. It may have seemed to Mary that this was all of a piece with an idyllic life in France. But in the background the shadows of politics and violence were already gathering. Whatever the affection of Mary and Francis, their marriage was a political one. Henry II wanted to secure French interests in Scotland, and hoped to unite the French and Scottish crowns by this match, so making Scotland merely a French satellite. The Scots were naturally concerned to preserve their own customs and their independence. The public marriage treaty guaranteed this; but in a secret marriage treaty, Mary, perhaps too young to realize quite what was at stake, or too French to care, signed away Scotland to the French. When a number of the Scottish commissioners who had come to witness her marriage died mysteriously on their way home, and word of the secret treaty leaked out, it was suspected that they might have known too much, and been murdered because of it.

That November, the death of Mary of England heralded the end of England's brief return to Roman Catholicism. Elizabeth, her half-sister, succeeded to the throne. Such was Henry's tangled matrimonial history, that in disentangling himself from Anne Boleyn, Elizabeth's mother, he had bastardized

Mary Queen of Scots

Elizabeth. If Elizabeth were a bastard, then the rightful sovereign of England was Mary Queen of Scots, by virtue of a Tudor grandmother. Henry II encouraged his daughter-in-law to assert her claim, and to wear the Royal Arms of England. It was advice Mary would follow to her ultimate peril.

The following June disaster struck France. Henry II was fond of jousting. He arranged a tournament for that month. The sport began as planned. The king and his opponent broke their lances on each other's armour. However, when Henry insisted on another bout, a freak accident caused a splinter of his opponent's lance to get past his visor, and pierce his eye. Though he lived for ten more agonizing days, the splinter had penetrated the brain.

Mary, besides being Queen of Scots and claiming to be Queen of England, was now Queen Consort of France. The moment of the Guises had come. They had, however, one particularly serious rival for power. Catherine de' Medici had never won much popularity for herself in France. For one thing, she was not royal-born, and was only allowed to marry into the French royal family at a time when it was not expected that her husband would ever succeed to the throne. However, she had a royal appetite for power.

The Guises had good cause to be wary of her. Their royal influence hung by the thread of Francis's none too sturdy life. Should he die before Mary had given birth to an heir, the Guises would have to plan afresh. The crown would pass to Francis's brother, Charles, over

Francis II of France

whom Catherine exerted greater influence. Indeed, Charles's sanity was precarious, and it is said that Catherine exploited this mental instability to make her son cripplingly dependent upon her. Francis, on whom Mary lavished protective affection, apart from being sickly, was probably physically incapable of fathering a child.

Beset as she was with ambitious and unscrupulous people, it was a blow to Mary when her mother died in June 1560. As would happen several times in her life, emotional strain prostrated her. But worse was in store. Francis's health was worsening. On 5 December he died, and Mary withdrew from the court to observe the prescribed 40 days of mourning. When she re-emerged it was hard to see what could detain her in

France any longer. She was no longer Queen of France, but she was still Queen of Scotland. Her Guise uncles may have entertained schemes in which she should marry the new king, but responsibilities to her kingdom dictated her departure, whether she personally wanted it or not.

Mary in white mourning for Francis

RETURN TO SCOTLAND

Mary's return to the country over which she had reigned in name since shortly after her birth, was lacklustre. She was accustomed to the luxury and ceremony of the French court, and to its language and culture. She was half French, and if anywhere was home for her, it was France. But Catherine de' Medici was in control of France, and some stories tell of the older woman's bitter resentment of the young and charming Queen. Possibly it suited

Catherine that Mary, who had been such a useful instrument to her Guise relatives, should go back whence she came.

From the first the omens were bad. As Mary boarded her ship, another vessel in the harbour capsized and its occupants were drowned. By a stroke of irony, the commander of Mary's little fleet was one of her future husbands, James Hepburn, Earl of Bothwell, a man destined to shake the ship of the Scottish state, and contribute to the overthrow of its sovereign.

At Leith, where she stepped ashore, she found a cool welcome. She was unexpected, and was greeted only by a few fisherfolk. She lodged at an ordinary town house, somewhat beneath her queenly dignity, while arrangements were made to carry her to Edinburgh. Those arrangements proved to consist of a horse that looked fit for nothing but the knacker's yard. *En route*, she made herself popular by pardoning a man who had been sentenced to death for frivolity on the Sabbath. But in doing so she confirmed the suspicions of the fanatical Protestant preacher, John Knox, that she was an enemy of his religion. Knox was a force to be reckoned with in Scotland. A former Catholic priest, now zealously anti-Catholic, and possessed of an unshakeable conviction of his own righteousness and destiny, Knox could seem at times almost a caricature of a reformer. He was an enthralling preacher, although his time in the galleys from 1547 to 1549 had done nothing to sweeten his temper, or make him a jot more tolerant of his enemies. His enemies

John Knox preaching against Mary

were the Lord's enemies; the Lord's enemies were evil. The Scotland to which Mary now returned was divided into factions in various ways – by family and clan, by geography, and perhaps most importantly, by religion. Such divisions made the political situation dangerous and unstable. It would call for the coolest, boldest and practised leadership.

One man in Scotland who did possess these qualities in some degree was Mary's half-brother, James Stewart. He was one of James V's many bastards, and chafed at the circumstance of his birth, which deprived him of the crown and settled it upon the head of a slip of a girl. However, he concealed his ambitions for the time being, and presented himself to Mary as a loyal friend.

James was a Protestant, which endeared him
to his co-religionists. However, he was happy
to let Mary celebrate Mass at Holyrood
House, her palace in Edinburgh, and make
for herself there a little oasis of French court
culture. Even though he personally had to
intervene to save the lives of her priests when
an anti-Catholic mob went on the rampage, it
suited him that his half-sister should make
herself unpopular with the Protestants.

Mary, in her innocence, thought it would be
pleasant if all her subjects, Catholic and
Protestant alike, could agree to live and let
live; however, as yet she lacked the political
acumen to judge how far it would be possible
to pursue such a policy. Of the guile that was
a necessary political tool, she then had little.
She agreed to meet John Knox in the hope of

arriving at an understanding. It was a forlorn
hope. Mary ended up compromising her regal
status by letting Knox lecture her and evade
her questions. Queen Elizabeth of England
would never have permitted such insolence.
Mary could not silence criticism of her court
and herself. Her French, Catholic way of life
went on, with such elegant amusements as a
cross-dressing masque, which, no matter how
innocent, put a stick into the hand of Knox
and his followers with which to beat her.
There was perhaps no more licentiousness at
Mary's court than in the household of many a
Protestant nobleman, but what there was was
eagerly seized on. So Mary's subjects came to
hear of the scandal of a servant who had given
birth to an illegitimate child, and then killed
it. Father and mother were duly punished for
their hideous crime. When a French poet hid

Mary's bedroom in Holyrood House

twice in the Queen's bedchamber, apparently intending to make love to her, he too was punished: he was tried for treason and executed. If such severity was meant to prove Mary's probity, it failed to do so. To her foes it all merely confirmed that the court was a hellish place of lust and bloodshed.

DARNLEY AND RIZZIO

It was Mary's misfortune that she lived her life surrounded by ruthless, selfish, and unpleasant men. It was a further blow that, by up-bringing and temperament, she needed love and reassurance, and had one talent by which to win them: her now legendary charm. But hers was no world in which to depend on the kindness of strangers. To the Scottish noble-men who gathered about her, she represented an opportunity. The man who wed her could become in practice, and perhaps, in title, King of Scotland.

In the midst of the factional jockeying for position, between Catholics and Protestants, Highlanders and Lowlanders, or just between feuding families, it was natural that Mary should seek solace from those who had nothing to do with the situation. One such was David Rizzio. He was an Italian musician, whose talents and continental culture recommended him to her, and who rose through Mary's household to become her secretary.

Mary sought something more than an urbane servant, however. She wanted romance. She selected as the object of her affection Henry Stuart, Lord Darnley, son of the Earl of

Lord Darnley

Lennox, and with royal Scottish and English blood flowing in his veins. He was a handsome if somewhat immature-looking young man. While he thought he had anything to gain he could be charming enough; and in the Queen of Scotland he had everything to gain. Marriage to her would bring him and his family great power. Mary was soon infatuated with him. She gave him costly gifts, and she clothed him head to toe in the most lavish attire. Thus adorned, for the time being Darnley was the apple of her eye. Oblivious to the annoyance of her powerful half-brother, James (now Earl of Moray), and of Protestant nobility, Mary pressed ahead with the marriage, which was solemnized on 29 July 1565.

Trouble was not far behind. Moray rebelled.

The rebellion was put down, but with little help from Darnley, who, notwithstanding having acquired the title King of Scotland, showed himself more concerned for his family than the kingdom by insisting that military command be given to Lennox, who was manifestly not the best person for the job.

The rebellion dealt with, Mary confronted problems even closer to home. Darnley may have had something of the charm of gilded youth, but it came with a childish, callow arrogance which now made itself felt. Determined to have his own way, he would be petulant and peevish if thwarted. Having got Mary, he was less inclined to charm her, and his faults became clear to her. He drank heavily, was absurdly overbearing, and whored his way around Edinburgh.

Medallion celebrating Mary and Darnley's marriage

The Protestant lords had suffered a setback with Moray's defeat. Now they saw a chance to reassert themselves, and use Darnley as a mask for their real motives. They had long disliked Rizzio: he was a Catholic, he was foreign, and they leapt to the conclusion that he must be a spy for a Catholic power intent on conquering Scotland and reimposing Catholic uniformity. They would be glad of the chance to murder him. However, they also wanted Darnley in on the plot, so they persuaded him that Rizzio had cuckolded him. Thus the assassination could be presented as a matter of honour, while Mary would get the message that she could not afford to displease the conspirators.

On the evening of 9 March, Mary, who was pregnant, was having an informal supper in her apartments at Holyrood. Rizzio was in attendance. The conspirators burst in upon her, Lord Ruthven, then mortally ill, cutting a particularly ominous figure, clad in armour with his deathly face under a helmet. They demanded that Rizzio come away with them. Terrified, Rizzio clung to the Queen, but was snatched away. Darnley restrained his wife, while Rizzio was hauled, writhing, from the room to a gruesome death from some fifty dagger thrusts.

Imminent danger cleared Mary's head. As she heard Rizzio's death-screams, she determined on vengeance. She had been taken prisoner in her own palace, and had to escape. She had once been infatuated with Darnley, but now she knew his weaknesses only too well – well enough to exploit them. The reality of bloodshed had already done something to shake Darnley out of the egotistical delusion that the evening's proceedings were mainly concerned with his honour. Manifestly, the conspirators were pursuing their own agenda, on which Darnley did not figure very highly. He was frightened enough for his loyalty to waver. Mary talked him round. To escape, they would have to have the soldiers who had been sent to guard her dismissed. This she did by claiming that, in her pregnant condition, she found them disturbing. Darnley was left as her sole guard overnight. The Queen and Darnley slipped away across a burial ground to waiting horses, and then on to Dunbar Castle.

BOTHWELL AND DARNLEY

Foremost among those who rallied to her cause was the Earl of Bothwell – the same man who had escorted Mary back from France. Bothwell's was a turbulent, active nature. He was possessed of enormous lust and ambition, though he was also a patriot. With him at her side, on 18 March Mary re-entered Edinburgh with a force of 8000 men. The conspirators fled. There, on 19 June

Lord Bothwell

1566, she gave birth to a son, James, who was destined to be King of Scotland and eventually of England.

In the short term this did little to strengthen her position. James would be likely to be brought up a Catholic, and so Protestant nobles would have everything to lose by letting events take their course. Her position was still very fragile. Outwardly she was reconciled with Darnley, but if he was a poor husband, he was a worthless statesman, with a talent for incurring resentments he could not handle. While Darnley was no support, Mary was hardly a pillar of strength herself. Under immediate threat, she'd shown spirit and presence of mind. The danger passed, but the underlying problems of her position unsolved, she fell prey to illness and deep depression. By the end of the year the French Ambassador was recording that she was ill, and reporting, 'I do believe the principal part of her disease to consist in a deep grief and sorrow . . . Still she repeats these words, "I could wish to be dead".'

However, her interest in life was soon to be revived – though by questionable means. Bothwell had been instrumental in keeping Mary on her throne. The comparison between Darnley and Bothwell, had Mary cared to make it, must have been in Bothwell's favour. Where Darnley was weak and fickle, Bothwell was strong and patriotic – though in other respects, especially as regards women, utterly unscrupulous. He had a huge sexual appetite that he saw no reason not to gratify. To some extent this was a family trait. He had been brought up in the household of his great-uncle, the Bishop of Moray, a notorious womanizer. Nor did the family confine itself to exercising *droit de seigneur*: it was virtually a tradition that a Hepburn offer widowed Queens such consolation as the flesh affords. Bothwell's own father had got divorced in order to marry Mary's mother, though the wedding never took place. Bothwell personally was a compelling figure: the best surviving likeness of him is a miniature which shows a face framed by dark hair, set off by a small dark beard, turning away into the shadow from which hooded, troubled eyes gaze out at us (though he had lost one eye by the time he met Mary). It's a far stronger face than Darnley's, but it also hints at the inner turbulence that would finally cost him his sanity. Mary may well

have found this difficult, powerful man
interesting. For his part, a closer liaison with
the Queen held obvious attractions, and
clearly Darnley was no longer much of a rival
for her affections.

He was, however, an obstacle. That he
himself had recently married Jean Gordon,
sister to the powerful Earl of Huntly, would
not have troubled Bothwell overmuch. But
while Mary remained married to Darnley, his
ambitions were stymied. Darnley had to leave
the picture, either by divorce or by death.

By the time the plot was hatched which,
however clumsy, would deprive him of his
life, Darnley was in a sorry state. He had
contracted syphilis, which made him stink,
and obliged him to wear a gauze mask, so

unsightly had this once handsome youth become. He had been taken ill in Glasgow at the end of 1566. But in January Mary brought him back to Edinburgh and lodged him in a house in a quadrangle known as Kirk o' Field. Twice during the ten days Darnley was to spend there, Mary slept in the room below his. On the night of 9 February she was to have done so again, but was detained at Holyrood. At about 2.00 a.m. the house was shattered by a huge explosion. Two of Darnley's servants were found dead in the rubble. The bodies of Darnley and his valet were found in the garden, scantily clad – Darnley's especially – but quite unscathed.

The exact nature of Mary's part in all this is impossible to determine – not least because it is impossible to know exactly what happened anyway. Theories abound, and the waters are muddied still further by the alleged evidence of the Casket Letters, later produced by her enemies and purporting to demonstrate that she had colluded with Bothwell in her husband's murder. The crucial passages of the letters are likely to have been doctored to incriminate her. It's equally difficult to know the exact nature of her relationship with Bothwell at this stage. Even if they were lovers, that doesn't necessarily make Mary guilty of Darnley's murder. If she were pregnant by Bothwell, she might have decided to stage a reconciliation with Darnley to make it seem that the child was legitimate. She did indeed miscarry twins on 24 July 1567, though it's impossible to know by how many months she was pregnant at the time. If there's anything in this theory, then Mary would have wanted Darnley alive. Bothwell, however, might well have wanted Darnley out of the way. But the crime is still fraught with mystery. There is, for example, the problem of the sheer size of the explosion. If the conspirators, whoever they were, merely wanted to kill Darnley, blowing up a robustly built stone house to do it was taking a heavy sledgehammer to crack a small nut. Why not just poison him, and claim that he had succumbed to his illness? Besides, the explosion seems unlikely to have been the cause of death, given that his body was found unmarked, albeit quite dead. Possibly the plan went wrong, Darnley got wind of it, ran from the house as he was, and was stifled outside. No one from that day to this has been able to solve the crime of Kirk o' Field.

Her enemies later made much of Mary's alleged complicity in her husband's murder. But at the time, what scandalized Europe and robbed her of respect, was not what she might or might not have done about Darnley, but what she went on to do about Bothwell. In the immediate wake of the murder she seems to have suffered a breakdown. Was this a queasy conscience? Or was it a perfectly innocent woman reflecting that the explosion might have been meant to kill her? Whatever its cause, it seems unlikely that she was heart-broken at Darnley's loss in itself.

Bothwell was such an obvious suspect that he stood trial for the crime. However, the prosecution was left in the hands of Lennox, and Bothwell so filled Edinburgh with his own supporters that Lennox didn't dare enter the city. Bothwell was therefore acquitted on 12 April. A week later he secured the pledge of 8 bishops and 21 nobles to support his marriage to Mary. They were later to claim that Bothwell had forced them to sign the bond, but it is just possible that some of them saw in Bothwell the kind of boldness and resolution needed to lead Scotland. Just five days later that boldness was manifested when he seized the Queen and carried her off to Dunbar Castle. There, in a move characteristic of the man, he raped her. It was a daring, self-advertising gesture. The extent of Mary's complicity in these arrangements is uncertain. It seems likely that she knew of at least part of the plan in advance. In later years she told different versions of the story, and it's conceivable that her life was in such turmoil that she herself was unclear as to exactly what she had done. The idea that Bothwell and Mary would now have to marry established itself.

The following month Bothwell set about extricating himself from his marriage. His wife countered by bringing an action against him for adultery with a serving girl. In the blaze of such unsavoury publicity, Bothwell and Mary married on 15 May 1567.

The marriage may have pleased Bothwell and Mary for a while, though, *pace* those who claim she found hitherto untasted sexual satisfaction in it, she never spoke of it as anything other than a political match. It certainly pleased nobody else. To Protestants it was further evidence of her immorality. In the eyes of Catholics all over Europe, including the Pope, marriage to a divorced Protestant discredited Mary. It's possible that not even the principals derived much joy from the union: even before the ceremony they were reported to be out of humour with each other.

Whether they shared happiness or misery, they did not share it for long. Forces were swiftly gathered to oppose them. Their enemies were united by the objective of parting Mary and Bothwell as by little else. The question was in whose interests would this coalition be directed? The two forces finally met at Carberry Hill. For a day they faced each other. There was some attempt at negotiation, and an offer from Bothwell to settle the matter by single combat. Mary's army began to lose heart and drift away to the other side. She decided to come to terms with her enemies before it was too late, and negotiated Bothwell's freedom on the condition that she go back to Edinburgh.

They never met again. Bothwell went first to Dunbar. Hearing that the charge of murdering Darnley had been revived, he realized he needed a power-base, and finally went north to the Orkneys, the Dukedom of which Mary had conferred on him. There he sought to assemble a naval force capable of annoying his enemies. But they again proved stronger, and Bothwell was forced to flee to Norway. He never regained the initiative. He had the bad luck to run into a woman he'd deserted years before, who threatened him with an action for breach of promise. From there he went to Denmark, where he dwindled to being a pawn in a diplomatic game, in which the Danish king hoped to gain the Orkneys and the Shetlands. While Bothwell looked as if he might be of some use, he was well treated. Once that moment had passed, he was cast into a cell, chained up, and left to rot. Insanity overtook him and it is said he used to dash himself against the walls. He died in 1578.

Mary's son, James, as a child

CONFINEMENT AND ESCAPE

Mary's captors carried her from Carberry, inflicting on her such humiliations as they could devise. In Edinburgh two soldiers carried before her a banner showing the body of Darnley and the infant James, calling on God to avenge his father's death. Crowds called for her blood. She was even forced to go via Kirk o' Field before lodging in the Provost's House. There she was kept for a

night and a day, until fear and anxiety over-
came her, and in a fit she tore madly at her
own clothes. Then she was escorted to Holyrood.

She was not to enjoy these more familiar
surroundings for long. From Holyrood she
went almost immediately to Lochleven in
Kinross-shire. This was the place picked out
for her incarceration. Moray, her half-
brother, was the chief of those who gained
by her defeat. Lochleven was presided over
by the Douglases, Sir William and his
mother, Margaret Erskine, who had been
mistress to James V and was also Moray's
mother.

The forces ranged against Mary appeared
strong, but they had problems of their own.

The desire to part Mary from Bothwell had united them. That to a large extent was now done, and many would have been happy to revert to their traditional loyalty to their rightful sovereign. But the initiative was seized by a more radical faction, who wanted Mary to abdicate in favour of her son, James, so that real power would pass to Moray, who would become regent.

Pressure was applied to this end. Moray himself came to Lochleven to promote his cause. Mary capitulated, though she must have known that a forced abdication could always be revoked. In the country at large, support for her remained surprisingly strong, as events would show. The kind of usurpation Moray sought to confirm was a comparative rarity in Scottish history. It was usually a safe assumption that a reigning monarch would resume power.

Lochleven was, as its name implies, in the middle of a loch. While she was not kept in harsh conditions, escape was no simple matter. However, Mary had a secret weapon: her fabled charm. It made her allies of George Douglas, Sir William's son, and Willie, an orphaned cousin. According to one story, a doomed escape attempt involved Mary dressing up as one of the washerwomen who took the household's laundry to the mainland to be washed. It was a somewhat unlikely ploy since Mary was particularly tall for a woman. In the end, however, it was not her height, but the whiteness of her hand that gave her away. The boatman, seeing hands of unusual whiteness and delicacy, was eager to see more of this well-muffled figure. He pressed his point, only to find he had been ogling his Queen.

The next attempt, planned by Willie, fared better. A May Day feast was arranged, in which he would enjoy the privileges of a Lord of Misrule, and would have the right to order everyone to do silly or unlikely things. He exercised his right, and ordered Mary from the hall. He still had to get his hands on Sir William's keys. Sir William always kept them by him. Even now they were by his plate on the table. Willie had, however, plied the head of the family with alcohol, just enough so that when he casually dropped his napkin over the keys, and picked it up with the keys concealed inside it, Sir William failed to notice. Willie joined the Queen, and they walked out of the castle, locking the gate behind them. Willie had earlier taken the precaution of tying up all the boats, bar one, to hinder pursuit. In this boat they now made good their escape.

Mary had been a prisoner for eleven months. For the next eleven days she was again a queen in fact as well as name. With astonishing speed she rallied a force of 5000-6000 men – no small feat considering that they can have had no warning of her escape. Her force continued to grow, and it seemed it would be just a matter of time before she could put an army in the field that would rout Moray's. However, she did not wait long enough for forces from the Highlands to join her. It's possible that Lord Hamilton was over-anxious to give battle, to preserve his prominence among the Queen's supporters, before too many powerful rivals had joined her cause. He was already annoyed to have been passed over as commander in favour of the Earl of Argyll. For whatever reason, Mary fought too soon.

Moray's army, under the capable command of Kirkcaldy numbered only 4000. Even so, Kirkcaldy managed to select both the time and place of battle, and inflicted a defeat on Mary at Langside on 13 May 1568.

Her army was routed, but by the standards of the time not very many had been killed. Arguably, Mary's best course would have been to regroup her forces, gather reinforcements, and try again. Instead she lost her head, and decided to flee the country. Worse folly was yet to come. Instead of going to France, where she would at least have had her powerful Guise relatives to assist her, she went to England. On 16 May she slipped across the Solway in a small boat and landed in Cumberland, in Elizabeth's kingdom.

MARY AND ELIZABETH

Mary wrote to Elizabeth as 'my dearest sister', asking to be conducted to her presence. They were never to meet. Yet Elizabeth could never afford to let her go. For the next nineteen years the two queens would play a game of cat-and-mouse – a game in which Elizabeth was always the cat, and Mary necessarily the mouse. At the time of her flight to England Mary was still only 25. Yet in those 25 years she'd done more living than

Queen Elizabeth

most manage in thrice the time. It was just as well: she wouldn't do much living from this point on. The most her active political life would amount to was the shadow-play of plot and counterplot.

In fleeing to England, Mary appears to have forgotten that she still lay claim to Elizabeth's throne. It also seems to have eluded her for the moment that, since she was a Catholic, and the new regime in Scotland was Protestant, Elizabeth would find it all but impossible to assist to regain her throne, for domestic reasons, if for no others, since England was also a Protestant country.

It was a little while before the extent of her folly dawned upon her. At first she fully expected to be welcomed by her sister

Queen. Elizabeth sent guards, ostensibly for Mary's protection, and moved her to Carlisle – the first of the many moves Elizabeth would order. Thither she sent her kinsman, Sir Francis Knollys.

Mary was a problem from the English point of view, a vexingly intractable one. In England she would become the focus of Catholic plots against Elizabeth; she was, after all, still heir presumptive to the English throne, even if one disallowed her earlier claim that it was already rightfully hers. She was also a potentially important figure in foreign affairs. If she were at liberty and went to France, and then regained her throne, the traditional Franco-Scottish alliance would revive to England's detriment. If she was allowed to go to Scotland, the same thing might happen, and the pro-

England faction in Scottish politics would lose out. Soon after her arrival, Sir William Cecil, Elizabeth's adviser, reviewed the evidence, and made the inconclusive comment: 'We find neither her continuance here good, nor her departing hence quiet for us.'

Elizabeth, who needed no encouragement to deal with awkward problems by postponing them, was swift to seize upon a pretext for inaction. Knollys relayed it to Mary: Elizabeth could not well meet her while she was still under a cloud of suspicion concerning her role in Darnley's demise. Elizabeth proposed an enquiry into the matter, at which Mary's Scottish accusers would be invited to submit evidence. Mary was encouraged to regard this as merely a prelude to her restoration with English support.

William Cecil

On 28 July Mary consented to the enquiry. It was always clear that Mary's guilt or innocence were not really what was at stake, however. The main issue concerned not justice, but politics. Mary was having to play a weak hand, but she did possess a few good cards. Her supporters were still fighting a civil war against Moray, and still seemed strong, although this was of limited use to Mary while she remained stuck in England. She was still a very desirable match, since, quite apart from her youth and that charm which many attested to, but which portraits do little to verify, she was Dowager Queen of France, Queen of Scotland, and next in line to the English throne, and divorce from Bothwell could readily be secured on the grounds of rape. She could also hold out to the English the possibility of conversion to Anglicanism, in which she did indeed express an interest, and promise to impose the Anglican brand of Protestantism as the official Scottish Church in the event of her restoration. This was not wholly implausible, since she had earlier shown some favour to the Reformed Church, and had, however disastrous the consequences, married a Protestant by a Protestant rite.

All these cards were in play when the enquiry opened at York on 4 October to investigate the narrower question of Mary's role in the murder of Darnley. Moray deemed it important enough to go to York himself to seek to discredit the half-sister he had deposed. While the proceedings were held in York, Mary fared quite well. She challenged her accusers, and scored a decided point against them on the broader issue of their support in Scotland, when she mentioned how few of the Scottish notables had attended James's coronation. However, on 3 November, Elizabeth transferred the hearings to West-minster and put them on a more formal footing. Moray continued to attend in person; Mary was not allowed to. As one of Cecil's agents put it, she had 'an alluring grace' – an alluring grace that Elizabeth did not intend to have revealed to the world at large.

Eventually, and understandably, Mary's representatives walked out of the hearings. Only then did Moray bring to light the allegedly damning evidence of the Casket Letters, when there was no one to challenge their authenticity. At the final session in December, Elizabeth unfairly blamed Mary's side for walking out on the proceedings, but drew the only conclusion she could draw, viz none at all. Both Moray and Mary were presumed innocent. Moray, however, went home with a £5000 loan; just over a year later he was assassinated. Mary remained in custody without trial.

Early in 1569 she was moved to Tutbury – one of several castles in which she would be kept, and the one she hated most. It was insanitary, damp and cold. Though she would be moved between Tutbury and Sheffield, with brief sojourns elsewhere, it was perhaps Tutbury that did most to undermine her health. She was still treated as a queen, with some 30 or 40 retainers, but her exercise was restricted compared with what it had been, and sources of excitement were few. The wearisome dullness of her days was not sufficiently alleviated by her hobby of embroidery, and so she turned to the thrills of plotting. Unfortunately for her there proved to be more embroidery than substance in the plots in which she implicated herself.

Various ruses were concocted. One was that she might marry the Duke of Norfolk, the senior peer of the realm. This was not so much treasonable as highly sensitive. More clearly criminal ideas were to follow. One such involved the Earls of Northumberland and Westmorland, who mounted a Catholic rebellion in 1569, in the course of which they tried to liberate Mary, and failed. As if anti-Catholic feeling in England were not running high enough, in February 1570 the Pope aggravated it by formally excommunicating

Elizabeth. This was soon followed by the Ridolfi plot, whose optimism was equalled only by its utter want of practicability: a foreign army was to topple Elizabeth, Mary was to marry Norfolk, and be settled on the thrones of England and Scotland. It came to nothing, but it cost Norfolk his life: he was executed in June 1572. The Massacre of St Bartholomew's Day in France later that year, in which thousands of French Protestants were put to death with the connivance of the government, fanned anti-Catholic sentiment still further, and many demanded that Mary share Norfolk's fate. But Elizabeth declined to execute Mary. It was doubtful whether she had the right to, and the execution of a queen would set a bad precedent.

For a time there was talk of Don John of

The Massacre of St Bartholomew's Day

Austria, the Spanish governor of the Nether-
lands, mounting an invasion of England,
marrying Mary, and ruling a united island
in her name. However, the plan was risky,
and was never attempted. Don John died in
1579.

The last few years of Mary's life saw a frenzy
of plotting, and bore out the prediction made
in 1572 by her brother-in-law, Charles IX of
France, that she would never stop plotting
until it had cost her her head. Mary sought a
Spanish invasion. The great invasion fleet of
the Armada, which finally sailed in 1588
showed that this was not a wholly unrealistic
hope. But even if it had come in time, and
had been successful, the Spanish would have
been unlikely to bow to Mary's interests.
Nevertheless, such castles in the air were a

pleasant, if dangerous, diversion from the
castles on the ground in which she was
imprisoned.

The only interruption to her intrigues was an
enforced one. Elizabeth sought a gaoler for
Mary who should be impervious to her
appeal, which, notwithstanding rheumatism
and other ailments, was still said to be
considerable. In Sir Amias Paulet she found
the right man. Paulet was a zealous Puritan,
and he brought his zeal to his work. When he
became Mary's gaoler, her secret corres-
pondence stopped. For a year she was incom-
municado.

In January 1586 Mary was delighted to find a
way to outwit the vigilance of her captors,
and she entered into secret communication

Mary, circa 1578

with plotters and would-be plotters again. Little did she know that she was the dupe of Elizabeth's spymaster, Sir Francis Walsingham. Walsingham served his Queen with such disinterested vigour that he financed his espionage network out of his own pocket. He had deliberately allowed Mary to open a channel of communication, by means of letters hidden in beer barrels, the better to spy upon her. Thus the Babington conspiracy was hatched in full view of Walsingham.

Anthony Babington was in his twenties, a secret Catholic, and, following a spell as Mary's page some years before, an admirer of hers. Unfortunately for her, his plan was not a jot more realistic than Ridolfi's. He aimed to rescue Mary (Mary had several suggestions about how to do this), murder Elizabeth, and establish Mary on the English throne, with the help of a rebellion and some foreign help. Unfortunately for Mary, she saw these plans, and approved them. That gave Walsingham the evidence he needed to destroy her. He searched her quarters, and seized her papers.

In a moment of black farce, Babington got wind of the danger he was in. Walsingham had ordered subordinates to invite Babington to dine with them and get him drunk in the hope that he would let slip valuable information or betray himself. Babington turned the tables on them by getting them drunk first, thus enabling him to snoop around. He found evidence that he was already under suspicion. Like Edgar in *King Lear*, he disguised himself as a wild beggar. However, after his uncharacteristic lapse, Walsingham returned to usual subtle form, and managed to lure Babington into a trap. He was tried with the rest of his conspirators. They were all executed, but the luckless Babington was one of just two to suffer the maximum penalty of being hanged, cut down while still alive, disembowelled, and quartered.

On 25 September Mary was transferred to Fotheringhay. The following month she was put on trial. She put up a dignified and spirited defence. She denied the competence of the court to try her, since she was not Elizabeth's subject and was a queen. She denied that she had been an accomplice in the part of the plot dealing with Elizabeth's death. The evidence, however, suggested otherwise. She was found guilty.

The sentence was for Elizabeth to decide. Even now she procrastinated, and sought some other way out of the problem. She tried to persuade Sir Amias Paulet to do away with his charge. But the man she had chosen for his probity gave an answer that was wholly in character: 'God forbid that I should make so foul a shipwreck of my conscience or leave so great a blot to my poor posterity, to shed blood without law or warrant.'

Finally, on 1 February 1587, Elizabeth signed Mary's death warrant. But she didn't send it. Instead, her secretary, William Davison, took it on his own initiative to the Privy Council, who dispatched it to Fotheringhay. Elizabeth seemed angry, genuinely or not, and had Davison imprisoned for a while.

But at last the decision was made.

The execution was set for 8 February. Mary was informed the previous evening. She put her affairs in order. In the small hours she wrote a letter to her brother-in-law, Henry III of France, complaining that she was to be executed in just a few hours 'like a criminal'. Early the following morning she proceeded to the hall with the small retinue that was all that Sir Amias would allow her. There she found a square platform, and on it the block.

For all her personal dignity, her death was marked by circumstances both grotesque and pathetic. Having heard the warrant read over, she laid her head upon the block. Bulle, the executioner, took two blows to sever it from her body. He then reached for the head to pick it up by the hair and show it to the assembled company, crying out 'God save the Queen'. Mary's lips were still moving, and went on doing so for a quarter of an hour. But what startled the company still more was that her hair came away in Bulle's hand, leaving her head, with short prematurely grey hair underneath the wig, to roll away. Somehow Mary's Skye terrier had managed to creep into the hall unnoticed, hidden in her skirts. It was now revealed, and in its loyalty and bewilderment took up a position between the head and the body and refused to be coaxed away. It later declined to eat and died.

So that Mary should not be seen as a martyr, every attempt was made to destroy anything

The execution of Mary

that might be regarded as a relic. Her clothes were burned; the block was burned; the normal executioner's perquisites were exchanged for money and destroyed. Even the hapless terrier was washed, lest he be thought to carry specks of his mistress's blood. Nothing of Mary should remain.

Except, of course, her story. And stories have a way of resisting the best efforts to cleanse and scour them out of existence. Mary's life had been an unlucky one, and she had occasionally compounded misfortune with folly. Little in her upbringing had prepared her for the complex and violent events that her birth decreed would be her lot. It's hard not to sympathize with her, and to feel the sincerity of her final instructions to her followers not to weep, but to 'rejoice that you see the end of the long troubles of Mary Stuart'. But the tales of her glories and miseries have fascinated everyone ever since.

FURTHER MINI SERIES INCLUDE

ILLUSTRATED POETS

Robert Burns
Shakespeare
Oscar Wilde
Emily Dickinson
Christina Rossetti
Shakespeare's Love Sonnets

FURTHER MINI SERIES INCLUDE

THEY DIED TOO YOUNG

Elvis
James Dean
Buddy Holly
Jimi Hendrix
Sid Vicious
Marc Bolan
Ayrton Senna
Marilyn Monroe
Jim Morrison

THEY DIED TOO YOUNG

Malcolm X
Kurt Cobain
River Phoenix
John Lennon
Glenn Miller
Isadora Duncan
Rudolph Valentino
Freddie Mercury
Bob Marley

FURTHER MINI SERIES INCLUDE

HEROES OF THE WILD WEST

General Custer
Butch Cassidy and the Sundance Kid
Billy the Kid
Annie Oakley
Buffalo Bill
Geronimo
Wyatt Earp
Doc Holliday
Sitting Bull
Jesse James